SUCCESSORIES
LIBRARY

The Power of Goals

Compiled by
Katherine Karvelas
Successories, Inc., Editorial Coordinator

CAREER PRESS
3 Tice Road, P. O. Box 687
Franklin Lakes, NJ 07417
1-800-CAREER-1; 201-848-0310 (NJ and outside U. S.)
FAX: 201-848-1727

THE POWER OF GOALS
Cover design by Successories
Typesetting by Eileen Munson
Printed in the U.S.A. by Book-mart Press

To order this title, please call toll-free 1-800-CAREER-1 (NJ and
Canada: 201-848-0310) to order using VISA or MasterCard, or for
further information on books from Career Press.

Library of Congress Cataloging-in-Publication Data

The power of goals : quotations to strengthen your climb to new
   heights / by editors of Successories.
        p.   cm.
    ISBN 1-56414-384-8 (pbk.)
    1. Goal (Psychology)--Quotations, maxims, etc.   I. Successories.
BF505.G6P68   1998
153.8--dc21
                                                          98-28304

Introduction

The search for personal and professional success is a lifelong journey of trial and error. This inspiring collection of wit and wisdom is a celebration of life's lessons. Each saying is a motivational push to stay on track of your goals and pursue your dreams.

In these pages you will find more than 300 powerful and compelling quotations from a diverse group of people—business professionals, writers, activists, actors, artists, sports professionals, scientists, philosophers, politicians, and everyday people who inspire us.

This unique collection was compiled after years of insightful reading and warm discussions with people who were kind enough to share their personal collections of quotations. Working on this book has been an enlightening and gratifying experience. We hope reading these quotes will be an equally gratifying and motivating experience for you on your journey of success.

The secret of success is constancy
of purpose.

Benjamin Disraeli

To achieve happiness, we should
make certain that we are never
without an important goal.

Earl Nightingale

The good man is the man who, no
matter how morally unworthy he
has been, is moving to become
better.

John Dewey

Goals are not only absolutely necessary to motivate us. They are essential to really keep us alive.

Robert H. Schuller

The world makes way for the man who knows where he is going.

Ralph Waldo Emerson

Your dreams grow holy put into action.

Adelaide Ann Procter

Progress has little to do with speed,
but much to do with direction.

Anonymous

Set positive goals and reasonable
expectations.

Steve Strasser

We all live with the objective of
being happy; our lives are all
different and yet the same.

Anne Frank

If we have not achieved our early dreams, we must either find new ones or see what we can salvage from the old. If we have accomplished what we set out to do in our youth, then we need not weep like Alexander the Great that we have no more worlds to conquer. There is clearly much left to be done, and whatever else we are going to do, we had better get on with it.

Rosalynn Smith Carter

Success in highest and noblest
form calls for peace of mind and
enjoyment and happiness, which
comes only to the man who has
found the work he likes best.

Napoleon Hill

When you determine what you
want, you have made the most
important decision in your life.
You have to know what you want
in order to attain it.

Douglas Lurtan

Goals that are not written down are just wishes.

Anonymous

Slight not what's near, while aiming at what's far.

Euripides

One's action ought to come out of an achieved stillness, not to be a mere rushing on.

D. H. Lawrence

Actually, all I ever wanted to be was
the best in my field.

Lou Holtz

Great minds have purposes, others
have dreams.

Washington Irving

No one can predict to what heights
you can soar, even you will not
know until you spread your wings.

Anonymous

If you are serious about your goals, drop the conditions. Go directly to your goal. Be your goal! Conditions often disguise strategies for escaping accountability. Why not just take charge and create the experience you are looking for.

Eric Allenbaugh

Life is a petty thing unless it is
moved by the indomitable urge to
extend its boundaries.

Jose Ortega y Gasset

Obstacles are those frightful things
you see when you take your eyes off
your goal.

Anonymous

A person can grow only as much as
his horizons allows.

John Powell

People with goals succeed because they know where they are going.

Earl Nightingale

The happiest excitement in life is to be convinced that one is fighting for all one is worth on behalf of some clearly seen and deeply felt good.

Ruth Benedict

Man can only receive what he sees himself receiving.

Floring Scovel Shinn

The only true happiness comes
from squandering ourselves for a
purpose.

John Mason Brown

If a man does not know what
port he is steering for, no wind
is favorable to him.

Anonymous

I finally figured out the only reason
to be alive is to enjoy it.

Rita Mae Brown

Those who are fired with an enthusiastic idea and who allow it to take hold and dominate their thoughts find the new worlds open for them. As long as enthusiasm holds out, so will new opportunities.

Norman Vincent Peale

Shoot for the moon. Even if you
miss, you'll land among the stars.

Anonymous

There is no giant step that does it.
It's a lot of little steps.

Peter A. Cohen

Why should I deem myself to be a
chisel, when I could be the artist?

Friedrich von Schiller

A life without cause is a life without effect.

Anonymous

I am a firm believer in the theory that the strongest motive, whether we are conscious of it or not, rules our conduct.

Ellen Glasgow

In whatever position you find yourself determine first your objective.

Marshal Ferdinand Foch

There does, in fact, appear to be
a plan.

Albert Einstein

Many persons have a wrong idea
of what constitutes true happiness.
It is not attained through
self-gratification, but through
fidelity to a worthy purpose.

Helen Keller

We must create our own world.

Louise Nevelson

It concerns us to know the purposes we seek in life, for then, like archers aiming at a definite mark, we shall be more likely to attain what we want.

Aristotle

You can't reach your goals without
occasionally taking some long
shots.

Anonymous

Your work is to discover your
work, and then with all your heart,
to give yourself to it.

Buddha

The mind determines what is
possible. The soul surpasses it.

Pilar Coolinta

Trust your hopes.

Anonymous

When we are motivated by goals
that have deep meaning, by
dreams that need completion, by
pure love that needs expressing,
then we truly live life.

Greg Anderson

Raise your hopes and expectations
high enough, and you shall touch
wings with the divine.

Celia Mora

There is no failure except in no longer trying.

Elbert Hubbard

Most of us serve our ideals by fits and starts. The person who makes a success of living is the one who sees his goal steadily and aims for it unswervingly.

Cecil B. DeMille

The occasion doesn't make the hero; it only discovers him.

Anonymous

The goal of civilization, all
religious thought, and all that
sort of thing is simply to have
a good time. But man gets so
solemn over the process that
he forgets the end.

Don Marquis

There is no achievement without goals.

Robert J. McKain

You, too, can determine what you want. You can decide on your major objectives, targets, aims, and destination.

W. Clement Stone

Make service your first priority, not success, and success will follow.

Anonymous

To have no set purpose in one's life
is the harlotry of the will.

Stephen MacKenna

Aim at the sun, and you may not
reach it; but your arrow will fly
higher than if aimed at an object
on a level with yourself.

Joel Hawes

It is not enough to aim; you must
hit.

Italian proverb

Without some goal and some effort
to reach it, no man can live.

Fyodor Dostoevsky

The most absurd and reckless
aspirations have sometimes led
to extraordinary success.

Vauvenargues

Today's preparation determines
tomorrow's achievement.

Anonymous

Aim at perfection in everything,
though in most things it is
unattainable. However they
who aim at it, and persevere,
will come much nearer to it
than those whose laziness and
despondency make them give it
up as unattainable.

Lord Chesterfield

First say to yourself what you would
be; and then do what you have
to do.

Epictetus

You measure the size of the
accomplishment by the obstacles
you had to overcome to reach
your goals.

Booker T. Washington

To win, you have to have the talent
and desire—but desire is first.

Sam Snead

A set definite objective must be
established if we are to accomplish
anything in a big way.

John McDonald

Always keep your ideals high
enough that you have to keep
stretching to reach them.

Anonymous

We are what and where we are
because we have first imagined it.

Donald Curtis

Goals are dreams with deadlines.

Diana Scharf Hunt

Continuity of purpose is one of
the most essential ingredients of
happiness in the long run, and for
most men this comes chiefly
through their work.

Bertrand Russell

You can plant a dream.

Anne Campbell

An intelligent plan is the
first step to success. The man
who plans knows where he is
going, knows what progress he
is making and has a pretty good
idea when he will arrive.
Planning is the open road to
your destination.

Basil S. Walsh

The purpose of life is a life of purpose.

Robert Byrne

Those who cannot tell what they desire or expect still sigh and struggle with indefinite thoughts and vast wishes.

Ralph Waldo Emerson

Desire and determination must overcome disappointment.

Walter Alston

The Power
of Goals

You must have long-range goals to
keep you from being frustrated by
short-range failures.

Anonymous

I hope that I may always desire
more than I can accomplish.

Michelangelo

I learned that if you want to make
it bad enough, no matter how bad
it is, you can make it.

Gale Sayers

The significance of a man is not what he attains but rather in what he longs to attain.

Kahlil Gibran

The first essential, of course, is to know what you want.

Robert Collier

The most important thing about goals is having one.

Geoffry F. Abert

We can do whatever we wish
to do provided our wish is
strong enough. What do you
want most to do? That's what
I have to keep asking myself,
in the face of difficulties.

Katherine Mansfield

The most important thing is to
have a code of life, to know how to
live. Find yourself a port of
destination.

Dr. Hans Seyle

The ultimate goal should be doing
your best and enjoying it.

Anonymous

Happiness is a direction, not a
place.

Sydney J. Harris

One half of knowing what you
want is knowing what you must
give up before you get it.

Sidney Howard

By asking for the impossible we
obtain the best possible.

Italian proverb

The great use of life is to spend it
on something that will outlast it.

William James

There is nothing worse than being
a doer with nothing to do.

Elizabeth Layton

You are the product of your own
brainstorm.

Rosemary Konner Steinbaum

Above all of single aim: Have a
legitimate and useful purpose, and
devote yourself unreservedly to it.

Anonymous

Our goals can only be
reached through a vehicle
of a plan, in which we must
fervently believe, and upon
which we must vigorously
act. There is no other route
to success.

Stephen A. Brennan

The men who succeed are the efficient few. They are the few who have the ambition and willpower to develop themselves.

Herbert N. Casson

If you aspire to the highest place, it is no disgrace to stop at the second, or even the third, place.

Cicero

Have the courage of your desire.

George Gissing

The big thing is that you know
what you want.

Earl Nightingale

Cherish your visions and your
dreams as they are the children of
your soul; the blue prints of your
ultimate achievements.

Napoleon Hill

Discipline is remembering what
you want.

David Campbell

High aims form high characters,
and great objects bring out great
minds.

Tyron Edwards

We must do the best we can with
what we have.

Edward Rowland Sill

We accomplish things by directing
our desires, not ignoring them.

Anonymous

*If one advances confidently
in the direction of his dreams,
and endeavors to live the
life which he has imagined,
he will meet with a success
unexpected in common hours.*

Henry David Thoreau

The trouble with not having a goal
is that you can spend your life
running up and down the field
and never score.

Bill Copeland

Goals determine what you're going
to be.

Julius Erving

Whoever wants to reach a distant
goal must take many small steps.

Helmut Schmidt

We are creators, and we can form
today the world we personally shall
be living in tomorrow.

Robert Collier

It takes a person with a mission
to succeed.

Clarence Thomas

Your success and happiness lie
in you.

Helen Keller

I never got a job I didn't create for myself.

Anonymous

The great thing in this world is not so much where we are but in what direction we are moving.

Oliver Wendell Holmes

Perfection is our goal, excellence will be tolerated.

Jay Goltz

The bravest are surely those who have the clearest vision of what is before them, glory and danger alike, and yet notwithstanding, go out to meet it.

Thucydides

If you set a goal for yourself and are able to achieve it, you have won your race. Your goal can be to come in first, to improve your performance, or just finish the race—it's up to you.

Dave Scott

Create mental pictures of your goals, then work to make those pictures become realities.

Anonymous

The Power
of Goals

Setting a goal is not the main thing. It is deciding how you will go about achieving it and staying with that plan.

Tom Landry

You have to expect things of yourself before you can do them.

Michael Jordan

Set your goals high, and don't stop till you get there.

Bo Jackson

The world stands aside to let
anyone pass who knows where
he is going.

David Starr Jordan

Life is a collection of self-fulfilling
prophecies.

John Nabor

Keep true, never be ashamed of
doing right; decide on what you
think is right, and stick to it.

George Eliot

The shortest and surest way
to live with honour in the
world is to be in reality what
we would appear to be; all
human virtues increase and
strengthen themselves by
the practice and experience
of them.

Socrates

It's not enough to be busy. The question is: What are we busy about?

Henry David Thoreau

To live means to have a mission to fulfill, and in the measure in which we avoid setting our life to something, we make it empty.

Jose Ortega y Gasset

Only he who can see the invisible can do the impossible.

Anonymous

To seek one's goals and to drive
toward it, stealing one's heart, is
most uplifting!

Henrik Ibsen

Lack of something to feel
important about is almost the
greatest tragedy a man may have.

Charles C. Nobel

Success is focusing the full power
of all you are on what you have a
burning desire to achieve.

Wilfred A. Peterson

Each of us has within us a life force,
a spirit, a principle, an essence, an
unfulfilled potential, that gives no
rest, no peace until it is realized.

Peter Nivio Zarlenga

Without a purpose nothing should
be done.

Marcus Aurelius

There can be no reality to the
things you want until they have
structure within your mind first.

Anthony Norvell

An aspiration is a joy
forever, a possession as solid
as a landed estate, a fortune
which we can never exhaust
and which gives us year by
year revenue of pleasurable
activity.

Robert Louis Stevenson

It's never finished. There's always
the next objective, the next goal.

Moya Lear

We must walk consciously only part
way toward our goal, and then leap
in the dark to our success.

Henry David Thoreau

Success is the progressive
realization of a worthy goal or
ideal.

Earl Nightingale

A man, as a general rule, owes very little to what he is born with—a man is what he makes of himself.

Alexander Graham Bell

The man who succeeds above his fellows is the one who early in life clearly discerns his object, and towards that object habitually directs his powers.

Edward George Bulwer-Lytton

Every great man has become
great, every successful man has
succeeded, in proportion as he
has confined his powers to one
particular channel.

Orison Swett Marden

Singleness of purpose is one of the
chief essentials for success in life,
no matter what may be one's aim.

John D. Rockefeller

Life's ups and downs provide windows of opportunity to determine your values and goals. Think of using all obstacles as stepping stones to build the life you want.

Marsha Sinetar

To make up your mind before you start that sacrifice is part of the package.

Richard M. Devos

You have to think big to be big.

Claude M. Bristol

Think little goals and expect little achievements. Think big goals and win big success.

David Joseph Schwartz

I was once asked if a big business
man ever reached his objective. I
replied that if a man ever reached
his objective he was not a big
business man.

Charles M. Schwab

The purpose of life is life.

Karl Lagerfeld

There is no happiness except
in the realization that we have
accomplished something.

Henry Ford

You must be single-minded. Drive
for the one thing on which you
have decided.

George S. Patton

All men seek one goal: success or
happiness.

Aristotle

Nothing can add more power to
your life than concentrating all of
your energies on a limited set of
targets.

Nido Qubein

The Power
of Goals

*Goals serve as a stimulus
to life. They tend to tap the
deeper resources and draw out
of life its best. Where there are
no goals, neither will there be
significant accomplishments.
There will only be existence.*

Anonymous

Nothing can resist the human will
that will stake even its existence on
its stated purpose.

Benjamin Disraeli

Cherish your visions, your ideals,
the music that stirs in your heart.
If you remain true to them, your
world will at last be built.

James Allen

It's time to start living the life we've
imagined.

Henry James

We must be the change we wish to
see in the world.

Gandhi

The tragedy of life doesn't lie in
not reaching your goal. The
tragedy lies in having no goal to
reach.

Benjamin Mays

Purpose is what gives life a
meaning.

C. H. Parkhurst

The poor man is not he who is
without a cent, but he who is
without a dream.

Harry Kemp

Those who have a "why" to live,
can bear with almost any "how."

Frank Victor

Every time you stand up for an
ideal, you send forth a tiny ripple
of hope.

Robert Kennedy

Far better it is to dare mighty
things, to win glorious triumphs,
even though checkered by failure,
than to take rank with those
poor spirits who neither enjoy
nor suffer much, because they
live in the grey twilight that
knows neither victory nor defeat.

Theodore Roosevelt

Unless you give yourself to some
great cause, you haven't even
begun to live.

William P. Merrill

Be a life long or short, its
completeness depends on what
it was lived for.

David Starr Jordan

An aim in life is the only fortune
worth finding.

Jacqueline Kennedy Onassis

You have to have a dream so you
can get up in the morning.

Billy Wilder

Many are stubborn in pursuit of
the path they have chosen, few in
pursuit of the goal.

Friedrich Nietzsche

Life has a value only when it has
something valuable as its object.

George Hegel

Our plans miscarry because they
have no aim. When a man does
not know what harbor he is
making for, no wind is the right
wind.

Seneca

Men cannot for long live hopefully
unless they are embarked upon
some unifying enterprise, one for
which they may pledge their lives,
their fortunes, and their honor.

C. A. Dykstra

Any individual can be, in time, what he earnestly desires to be, if he but sets his face steadfastly in the direction of that one thing and brings all his powers to bear upon its attainment.

J. Herman Randall

No pleasure philosophy, no
sensuality, no place nor power, no
material success can for a moment
give such inner satisfaction as the
sense of living for good purpose.

Minot Simons

A novelist must know what his last
chapter is going to say and one
way or another work toward that
last chapter. To me it is utterly
basic, yet it seems like it's a great
secret.

Leon Uris

There is one thing which gives radiance to everything. It is the idea of something around the corner.

G. K. Chesterton

A useless life is an early death.

Goethe

To grow and know what one is growing towards—that is the source of all strength and confidence in life.

James Baillie

There are three ingredients in the good life: learning, earning, and yearning.

Christopher Morley

If you cry "Forward," you must make plain in what direction to go.

Anton Chekov

Men, like nails, lose their usefulness when they lose direction and begin to bend.

Walter Savage Landor

You have to set the goals
that are almost out of reach.
If you set a goal that is
attainable without much
work or thought, you are
stuck with something below
your true talent and potential.

Steve Garvey

In everything one must consider
the end.

Jean de La Fontaine

Strong lives are motivated by
dynamic purposes.

Kenneth Hildebrand

One of the sources of pride in
being a human being is the ability
to bear present frustrations in the
interests of longer purposes.

Helen Merell Lynd

He turns not back who is bound to a star.

Leonardo da Vinci

Life has a meaning only if one barters it day by day for something other than itself.

Antoine de Saint-Exupery

He might never really do what he said, but at least he had it in mind. He had somewhere to go.

Louis L'Amour

If you want to succeed you should strike out on new paths rather than travel the worn paths of accepted success.

John D. Rockefeller

What most counts is not how to live, but to live aright.

Socrates

Choosing a goal and sticking to it changes everything.

Scott Reed

The principle goal of
education is to create men
who are capable of doing new
things, not simply of repeating
what other generations have
done—men who are creative,
and inventive.

Jean Piaget

No wind serves him who addresses
his voyage to no certain port.

Michel de Montaigne

Laboring toward distant aims sets
the mind in a higher key and puts
us at our best.

C. H. Parkhurst

Everything's in the mind. That's
where it all starts. Knowing what
you want is the first step toward
getting it.

Mae West

A straight path never leads
anywhere except to the objective.

Andre Gide

There's some end at last for the
man who follows a path; mere
rambling is interminable.

Seneca

Nothing contributes so much to
tranquilize the mind as a steady
purpose—a point on which the
soul may fix its intellectual eye.

Mary Shelley

The only people who attain power
are those that crave for it.

Erich Kastner

In this life we get only those things
for which we hunt, for which we
strive, and for which we are willing
to sacrifice.

George Matthew Adams

Destiny is not a matter of chance,
it is a matter of choice; it is not a
thing to be waited for, it is a thing
to be achieved.

William Jennings Bryan

The Power
of Goals

Think and feel yourself there!
To achieve any aim in life,
you need to project the end-result.
Think of the elation, the
satisfaction, the joy! Carrying
the ecstatic feeling will bring
the desired goal into view.

Grace Speare

There are two things to aim at in
life: first, to get what you want, and
after that to enjoy it. Only the
wisest of mankind achieve the
second.

Logan Pearsall Smith

We act as though comfort and
luxury were the chief requirements
of life, when all that we need to
make us really happy is something
to be enthusiastic about.

Charles Kingsley

You seldom get what you go after
unless you know in advance what
you want.

Maurice Switzer

A life that hasn't a definite plan is
likely to become driftwood.

David Sarnoff

Only he who keeps his eye fixed on
the far horizon will find his right
road.

Dag Hammarskjöld

Vision is the art of seeing the
invisible.

Jonathon Swift

Where no plan is laid, where the
disposal of time is surrendered
merely to the chances of incident,
chaos will soon reign.

Victor Hugo

Hitch your wagon to a star.

Ralph Waldo Emerson

O*f all the forces that make*

for a better world, none is

so indispensable, none so

powerful, as hope. Without

hope men are only half alive.

With hope they dream and

think and work.

Charles Sawyer

Far away in the sunshine are my
highest aspirations. I may not
reach them, but I can look up and
see the beauty, believe in them,
and try to follow where they lead.

Louisa May Alcott

One of the most important factors,
not only in military matters but
in life as a whole, is the ability to
direct one's whole energies towards
the fulfillment of a particular task.

Erwin Rommel

Every outlook, desirable or
undesirable, remains possible for
anyone, no matter what his present
outlook is.

Dr. George Weinberg

Concentrate on finding your goal,
then concentrate on reaching it.

Michael Friedman

There is nothing on earth you
cannot have—once you have
mentally accepted the fact that
you can have it.

Robert Collier

Enthusiasm for one's goal lessens
the disagreeableness of working
toward it.

Thomas Eakins

People can have many different
kinds of pleasure. The real one is
that for which they will forsake the
others.

Marcel Proust

Unhappiness is not knowing what
we want and killing ourselves to
get it.

Don Herold

The Power
of Goals

If you only care enough for a
result, you will almost certainly
attain it. Only you must, then,
really wish these things, and
wish them exclusively, and not
wish at the same time a hundred
other incompatible things just
as strongly.

William James

What our deepest self craves is
not mere enjoyment, but some
supreme purpose that will enlist
all our powers and give unity and
direction to our life.

Henry J. Golding

Concentrate all your thoughts on
the great desire in your life. This
concentration must be continuous,
unceasing—every minute; every
hour; every day; every week.

Charles E. Popplestone

The most powerful factors in the
world are clear ideas in the minds
of energetic men of goodwill.

J. Arthur Thompson

Unless you try to do something
beyond what you have already
mastered, you will never grow.

Anonymous

High achievement always takes
place in the framework of high
expectations.

Jack Kinder

Not only must we be good, but we must be good for something.

Henry David Thoreau

Those who attain any excellence commonly spend life in one pursuit; for excellence is not often granted upon easier terms.

Samuel Jackson

What's important is that one strives to achieve a goal.

Ronald Reagan

Set goals for yourself and work your hardest to achieve them. Some goals you will achieve and others you won't, but at least you will have the satisfaction of knowing where you were going.

Beth Daniel

Pursue worthy aims.

Solon

To have reason to get up in the morning, it is necessary to possess a guiding principle. A belief of some kind. A bumper sticker, if you will.

Judith Guest

Having a goal is a state of happiness.

E. J. Bartek

The sky is the limit when your
heart is in it.

Anonymous

There is only one meaning in life:
the act of living itself.

Erich Fromm

Happiness is essentially a state of
going somewhere, wholeheartedly,
one-directionally, without regret or
reservation.

William H. Sheldon

He who labors diligently need
never despair; for all things are
accomplished by diligence and
labor.

Menander of Athens

Great hopes make the man.

Thomas Fuller

I believe half the unhappiness in
life comes from people being
afraid to go straight at things.

William J. Locke

There are those that travel
and those who are going
somewhere. They are different
and yet they are the same.
The success has this over his
rivals: He knows where he is
going.

Mark Caine

Fortunate is the person who has
developed the self-control to
steer a straight coarse toward his
objective in life, without being
swayed from his purpose by either
commendation or condemnation.

Napoleon Hill

Efforts and courage are not
enough without purpose and
direction.

John F. Kennedy

First make sure that what you
aspire to accomplish is worth
accomplishing, and then throw
your whole vitality into it.

B. C. Forbes

You must do the thing which you
think you cannot do.

Eleanor Roosevelt

The secret of living is to find the
pivot of a concept on which you
can make your stand.

Luigi Pirandello

An archer cannot hit the bullseye
if he doesn't know where the
target is.

Anonymous

Men must be decided on what they
will not do, and then they are able
to act with vigor on what they
ought to do.

Mencius

Big thinking precedes big
achievements.

Wilferd A. Peterson

Crystallize your goals. Make a plan for achieving them and set yourself a deadline. Then, with supreme confidence, determination and disregard for obstacles and other people's criticisms, carry out your plan.

Paul Meyer

Hold fast to your dreams, for if dreams die, then life is like a broken winged bird that cannot fly.

Langston Hughes

The task ahead is never as great as the power behind us.

Ralph Waldo Emerson

In the long run men hit only what they aim at.

Henry David Thoreau

To be what we are, and to become
what we are capable of becoming,
is the only end of life.

Baruch Spinoza

The aim of life is self-development,
to realize one's nature perfectly.

Oscar Wilde

All animals except man know
that the ultimate goal of life is to
enjoy it.

Samuel Butler

The very first condition of lasting
happiness is that a life should
be full of purpose, aiming at
something outside self.

Hugh Black

The business of life is to enjoy
oneself.

Norman Douglas

Man's reach should exceed his
grasp, or what's heaven for?

Robert Browning

Set goals in life; set them high and persist until they are achieved. Once they are achieved, set bigger and better goals. You will soon find that your life will become happier and more purposeful by working toward positive goals.

Raymond Floyd

Happiness is the overcoming of unknown obstacles toward a known goal.

L. Ron Hubbard

One never notices what has been done; one can only see what remains to be done.

Marie Curie

The true worth of a man is to be measured by the objects he pursues.

Marcus Aurelius

What lies behind us and what lies
before us are small matters
compared to what lies within us.

Ralph Waldo Emerson

Reach beyond your grasp. Your
goals should be grand enough to
get the best of you.

Pierre Teilhard de Chardin

To follow, without halt, one aim;
that's the secret of success.

Anna Pavlova

You begin by always expecting
good things to happen.

Tom Hopkins

The soul that has no established
aim loses itself.

Michel de Montaigne

When the mind of man can
conceive and believe, the mind of
man can achieve.

W. Clement Stone

If you have a goal in life that takes a lot of energy, that requires a lot of work, that incurs a great deal of interest and that is a challenge to you, you will always look forward to waking up to see what the new day brings.

Susan Polis Schultz

Limited expectations yield only
limited results.

Susan Laurson Willig

Aim at heaven and you get earth
thrown in; aim at earth and you
get neither.

C. S. Lewis

Nothing is more terrible than
activity without insight.

Thomas Carlyle

Every man is said to have his
peculiar ambition.

Abraham Lincoln

Follow your bliss. Find where it is
and don't be afraid to follow it.

Joseph Campbell

Ambition means longing and
striving to attain some purpose.
Therefore, there are as many
brands of ambition as there are
human aspirations.

B. C. Forbes

Few wishes come true by
themselves.

June Smith

Our children may learn about
heroes of the past. Our task is to
make ourselves architects of the
future.

Jomo Kenyatta

Once you say you're going to settle
for second, that's what happens to
you.

John F. Kennedy

W*e need to know where
we are going, and how we
plan to get there. Our dreams
and aspirations must be
translated into real and
tangible goals, with priorities
and a time frame.*

Merlin Olsen

Know your limits, but never stop
trying to exceed them.

Anonymous

The most effective way I know to
understand and clarify life purpose
is to develop a personal mission
statement.

Greg Anderson

Every calling is great when greatly
pursued.

Oliver Wendell Holmes

Our future will be determined by
our goals and by the struggle to
make them real.

Anonymous

No one knows what he can do till
he tries.

Syrus

Your vision will become clear only
when you look into your heart.
Who looks outside, dreams. Who
looks inside, awakens.

Carl Jung

When I dare to be powerful, to use
my strength in the service of my
vision, then it becomes less and less
important whether I am afraid.

Audre Lorde

The desire accomplished is sweet
to the soul.

Solomon

We are not in a position where we
have nothing to work with. We
already have capacities, talents,
direction, mission, callings.

Abraham Maslow

Whatever course you have chosen for yourself, it will not be a chore but an adventure if you bring to it a sense of the glory of striving, if your sights are set far above the merely secure and mediocre.

David Sarnoff

People begin to become successful
the minute they decide to be.

Harvey Mackey

The will to win is not nearly as
important as the will to prepare
to win.

Bobby Knight

You are never given a wish without
also being given the power to make
it true. You may have to work for it,
however.

Richard Bach

Here's the key to success and the key to failure: We become what we think about.

Earl Nightingale

Thoughts held in mind produce after their kind.

Anonymous

If today your abilities are small and your powers insignificant, begin now to make a more thorough use of them and they will grow.

Raymond Holliwell

The mode by which the inevitable
comes to pass is effort.

Oliver Wendell Holmes

You only grow by coming to
the end of something and by
beginning something else.

John Irving

The fact is, nothing comes; at
least nothing good. All has to be
fetched.

Charles Buxton

It is when things go hardest,
when life becomes most trying,
that there is the greatest need
for having a fixed goal. When
few comforts come from without,
it is all the more necessary to
have a fount to draw from
within.

B. C. Forbes

Every step you take should move
you in the direction of your vision.

Stephen C. Paul

Great thoughts speak only to the
thoughtful mind, but great actions
speak to all mankind.

Emily P. Bissell

Knowing is not enough, we must
apply; willing is not enough, we
must do.

Goethe

Yes, you can be a dreamer and a doer too, if you will remove one word from your vocabulary: impossible.

Robert Schuller

Genius begins great works; labor alone finishes them.

Joseph Joubert

There is no challenge more challenging than the challenge to improve yourself.

Michael F. Staley

These other Successories® titles are available from Career Press:

➤ *The Magic of Motivation*

➤ *The Essence of Attitude*

➤ *Commitment to Excellence*

➤ *Winning with Teamwork*

➤ *The Best of Success*

To order call: 1-800-CAREER-1

These other Successories® titles are available from Career Press:

➤ *Great Little Book on The Gift of Self-Confidence*

➤ *Great Little Book on The Peak Performance Woman*

➤ *Great Little Book on Mastering Your Time*

➤ *Great Little Book on Effective Leadership*

➤ *Great Little Book on Personal Achievement*

➤ *Great Little Book on Successful Selling*

➤ *Great Little Book on Universal Laws of Success*

➤ *Great Quotes from Great Women*

➤ *Great Quotes from Great Sports Heroes*

➤ *Great Quotes from Great Leaders*

➤ *Great Quotes from Zig Ziglar*

To order call: 1-800-CAREER-1